MONEY

·······FOR·······

HOBBIES

magic wagon

MARY ELIZABETH SALZMANN

Consulting Editor, Diane Craig, M.A./Reading Specialist

Paula Austin, B.A. Elementary Education/Math Consultant

visit us at www.abdopublishing.com

Published by Magic Wagon, a division of the ABDO Group,
8000 West 78th Street, Edina, Minnesota 55439.

Printed in the United States of America, North Mankato, Minnesota.
062010
092010

 This book contains at least 10% recycled materials.

Editor: Katherine Hengel
Content Developer: Nancy Tuminelly

Library of Congress Cataloging-in-Publication Data

Salzmann, Mary Elizabeth, 1968-
 Money for hobbies / by Mary Elizabeth Salzmann.
  p. cm. -- (Your piggy bank: a guide to spending & saving for kids!)
 ISBN 978-1-61641-030-8
 1. Money--Juvenile literature. 2. Hobbies--Costs--Juvenile literature. 3. Mathematics--Juvenile literature. I. Title.
 HG221.5.S265 2011
 332.024--dc22
                2009053779

What About Tax?

Given the audience and nature of this series, we chose not to directly address taxes as an element of an item's price. For the purposes of this series, the taxes are included in the prices!

CONTENTS

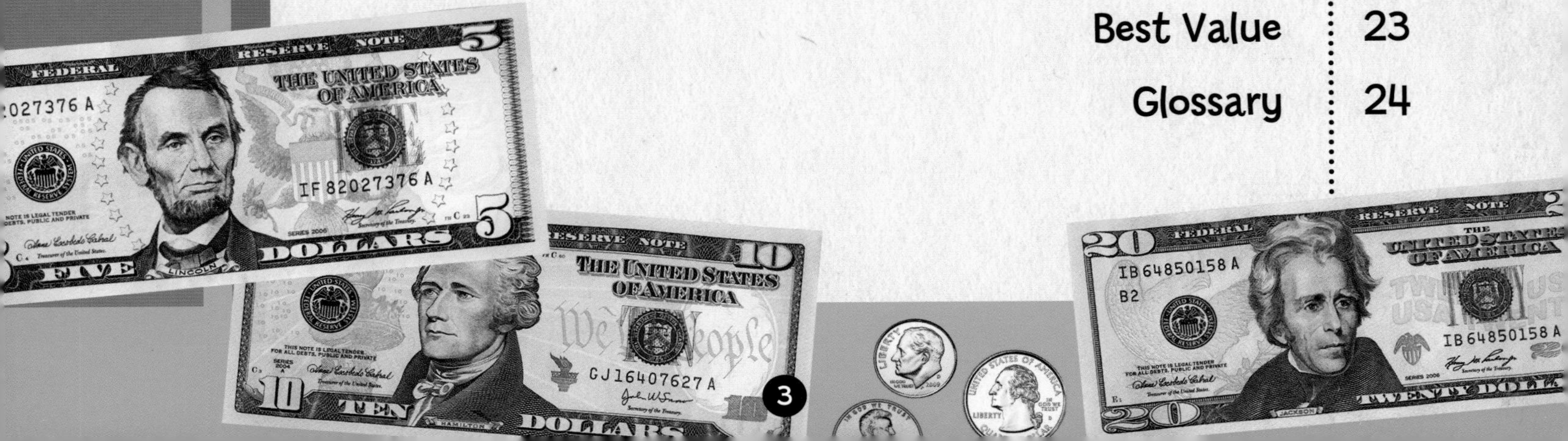

FEDERAL RESERVE NOTE
THE UNITED STATES OF AMERICA
IF 82027376 A
FIVE DOLLARS
THE UNITED STATES OF AMERICA
GJ 16407627 A
TEN DOLLARS
THE UNITED STATES OF AMERICA
IB 64850158 A
TWENTY DOLLARS
LIBERTY

COINS AND BILLS

PENNY		**ONE CENT**	1¢ or $0.01
NICKEL		**FIVE CENTS**	5¢ or $0.05
DIME		**TEN CENTS**	10¢ or $0.10
QUARTER		**TWENTY-FIVE CENTS**	25¢ or $0.25
DOLLAR BILL		**ONE DOLLAR** equal to one hundred cents	100¢ or $1.00

More Coins

There are also coins worth fifty cents and one dollar.

More Bills

Some bills are worth more than one dollar. Look for the number in the corners of a bill. That is how many dollars the bill is worth.

SPENDING MONEY

Here are some important ideas to think about when spending money.

Price
The price is how much you pay for something.

Quantity
The quantity is how many things you buy.

Quality
The quality of something is how well it is made or how well it works.

Value
Value is how price, quantity, and quality work together. It is good to think about value before you buy something.

Meet Emily!

Emily's parents give her money. She gets to decide what to buy. Follow along with Emily as she tries to make good decisions.

Emily's Goal

Emily wants to buy a new tennis video game. It costs **$10.00**. Her **goal** is to save enough money to buy the game!

Emily's Savings

Emily puts her savings in her piggy bank. She saves a little bit at a time. Small amounts can add up to a lot!

STAMPS

Emily collects stamps. Her parents give her some bills and coins to buy new stamps. How much money did they give her?

Organize the bills and coins into groups. Then add the groups together.

Find the total of each group. Then add the group totals together.

COUNT THE BILLS

There are three dollar bills.
3 dollars equal $3.00

Write the total of the bills.

$3.00

Add the first two groups.

$3.00
+$1.00

$4.00

GROUP COINS TO MAKE DOLLARS

There are ten dimes.
10 dimes equal $1.00

Write the total of the coins grouped in dollars.

$1.00

The sum of the first two groups is $4.00.

COUNT THE REST OF THE COINS

There are three quarters.
3 quarters equal 75¢

There are two nickels.
2 nickels equal 10¢

There are three pennies.
3 pennies equal 3¢

Find the total.
75¢ + 10¢ + 3¢ = 88¢

Write the total of the rest of the coins.

Write it in dollars, not cents.

$0.88 is the same as 88¢.

$0.88

Add the coins to the sum of the first two groups.

$4.00
+$0.88

$4.88

The total amount of all the bills and coins is **$4.88**.

Add It Up!

Emily's parents gave her $4.88 to buy stamps. Her aunt gave her another $1.00. Now how much money does Emily have?

I did the math on a piece of paper. You can see how I did it below. The total amount is $5.88.

Do the Math

Adding decimal numbers is a lot like adding whole numbers.

Line up the decimal points.

$4.88
+$1.00
———

Start from the right and add each column.

$4.88
+$1.00
———
8

Put a decimal point in the answer. It goes below the other decimal points.

$4.88
+$1.00
———
$5.88

Include the dollar sign in the answer.

Do the Math

Subtracting decimal numbers is a lot like subtracting whole numbers.

Line up the decimal points.

$$\begin{array}{r} \$5.88 \\ -\ \$4.21 \\ \hline \end{array}$$

Start from the right and subtract each column.

$$\begin{array}{r} \$5.88 \\ -\ \$4.21 \\ \hline 7 \end{array}$$

Put a decimal point in the answer. It goes below the other decimal points.

$$\begin{array}{r} \$5.88 \\ -\ \$4.21 \\ \hline \$1.67 \end{array}$$

Include the dollar sign in the answer.

Subtract It!

I can put $1.67 in my piggy bank! You can see how I figured it out at the top of the page.

Emily has $5.88 to buy stamps. She buys some stamps that cost $4.21. How much money does Emily have left?

Emily had $5.88. She spent $4.21. Now she has $1.67. Emily puts the leftover money into her piggy bank.

Emily's Piggy Bank

$$\begin{array}{r} \$0.00 \\ +\ \$1.67 \\ \hline \$1.67 \end{array}$$

ART SUPPLIES

Emily likes to draw. She needs a new **sketch** pad and some drawing tools. She can spend **$6.00** or less.

Which sketch pad and drawing tools should Emily choose?

$3.00

$4.50

$5.75

$1.50

$3.25

$4.00

Do the Math

Some of the combinations cost more than **$6.00**. Let's look at a couple of examples.

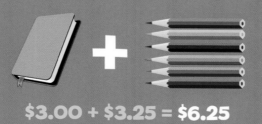

$3.00 + $3.25 = **$6.25**

$4.50 + $4.00 = **$8.50**

Decision Time

Emily has two **options**. She can buy the blue sketch pad and the crayons. Or, she can get the black sketch pad and the crayons. All the other combinations cost too much.

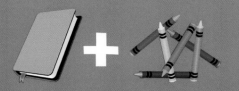

$3.00 + $1.50 = $4.50

$4.50 + $1.50 = $6.00

If Emily gets the black **sketch** pad and crayons, she will spend all her money. If she gets the blue sketch pad and crayons, she will still have $1.50! What will she choose?

> I'm going to get the blue sketch pad and the crayons. Then I can put $1.50 in my piggy bank!

Emily had $6.00. She spent $4.50. Now she has $1.50. Emily puts the leftover money into her piggy bank.

Emily's Piggy Bank

$1.67
+$1.50
—————
$3.17

11

Add It Up!

Emily also likes to paint. A set of paints costs **$1.92**. A paintbrush costs **$0.95**. What is the total cost of Emily's painting supplies?

$1.92

$0.95

I figured it out! It was easier when I wrote it down on paper. The total cost is **$2.87**.

Do the Math	Line up the decimal points.	Start from the right and add each column.	Regroup when digits in a column total ten or more.	Write the decimal point in the answer.
Adding decimal numbers is a lot like adding whole numbers.	$1.92 +$0.95	$1.92 +$0.95 ——— 7	1 $1.92 +$0.95 ——— 87	$1.92 +$0.95 ——— $2.87

Do the Math

Subtracting decimal numbers is a lot like subtracting whole numbers.

Line up the decimal points.	Start from the right and subtract each column.	Regroup as you would when subtracting whole numbers.	Write the decimal point in the answer.
$4.28 - $2.87	$4.28 - $2.87 —— 1	3 12 $4.28 - $2.87 —— 41	$4.28 - $2.87 —— $1.41

Subtract It!

Emily's parents give her $4.28 to buy painting supplies. She knows that the total cost is $2.87. How much money will she have left?

Emily had $4.28. She spent $2.87. Now she has $1.41. Emily puts the leftover money into her piggy bank.

> I can put $1.41 in my piggy bank! You can see how I figured it out at the top of the page.

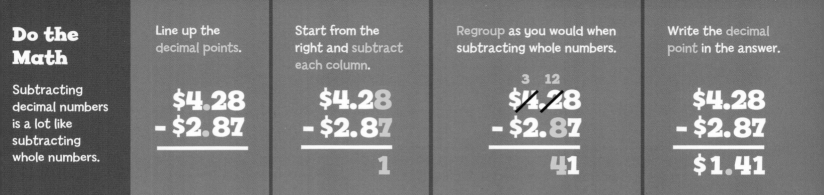

Emily's Piggy Bank

$3.17
+$1.41
——
$4.58

13

GOLF BALLS

Emily needs to buy golf balls for her next game. She can spend **$12.00** or less. Which golf balls should Emily buy?

$9.75

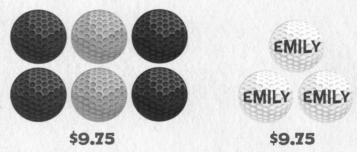

$9.75

$9.75

Think About It

To get the best value, she needs to think about price and quantity.

PRICE

All of the boxes of golf balls have the same price.

QUANTITY

The box of white golf balls has 12 balls.
The box of colored golf balls has 6 balls.
The box of **personalized** golf balls has 3 balls.

Decision Time

Emily can afford any of the golf balls. But she needs enough to last the whole game.

WHITE GOLF BALLS

There are 12 balls in the box of white golf balls. That is many more than the other boxes. Emily knows she'll need a lot of golf balls for the game.

COLORED GOLF BALLS

Emily thinks it would be nice to have colorful golf balls. But she doesn't think just 6 golf balls will last the whole game.

PERSONALIZED GOLF BALLS

Emily would love to have golf balls with her name on them. But she knows that 3 golf balls won't be enough.

The white golf balls are the best value. The others may be better looking. But there aren't enough for a whole game.

I'm going to buy the white golf balls. I'll get more for the same price.

Emily had **$12.00**. She spent **$9.75**. Now she has **$2.25**. Emily puts the leftover money into her piggy bank.

Emily's Piggy Bank

$4.58
+$2.25
———
$6.83

15

IT CAME FROM THE POND

Emily and her brother Adam are playing golf. Emily has twelve white balls. Adam bought the **personalized** golf balls, so he only has three. Who made the best decision? Let's see what happens!

AT THE THIRD HOLE

Emily made the best decision. She had enough golf balls to finish the game. And she didn't get dirty!

FISHING ROD

Emily entered a fishing contest! Her mom gave her **$15.00** to buy a new fishing rod. Emily wants one that will last. Which rod should she buy?

$7.00

$15.00

$10.00

Think About It

To get the best value, she needs to think about price and quality.

PRICE

The green rod has the lowest price. The red rod has the highest price.

QUALITY

Emily knows that the red rod is well made. It has the best quality. The green rod looks really flimsy. Emily doesn't think it would last very long. It has the worst quality.

Decision Time

Emily can afford any of the fishing rods. She thinks about each rod's price and quality.

THE GREEN ROD

The green rod has the lowest price. But it also has the worst quality. It would save Emily the most money. But it might break!

THE RED ROD

The red rod has the best quality. But it also has the highest price. It would be a great rod to have. But Emily would have to spend all her money.

THE BLUE ROD

The blue rod has a low price and good quality. Emily won't have to spend all her money, *and* she'll have a great fishing rod!

The green fishing rod isn't good enough. Emily doesn't like its quality.

The red rod is too expensive. Emily doesn't want to spend that much.

Emily thinks the blue rod is good enough. And it doesn't cost a lot either!

I'm going to buy the blue rod. Then I'll have $5.00 to put in my piggy bank!

Emily had $15.00. She spent $10.00. Now she has $5.00. Emily puts the leftover money into her piggy bank.

Emily's Piggy Bank

$6.83
+$5.00
———
$11.83

THE CASE OF THE LUCKY FISH

Choosing the cheapest thing isn't always the best idea. Usually, the less something costs, the worse its quality is. Saving money might not be worth it if what you buy doesn't work.

Lauren's "lucky" rod wasn't so lucky after all! It looks like Emily made a better decision.

SAVING UP!

Emily's **goal** was to buy a tennis video game for $10.00. She saved a little bit of money at a time. Finally, she was able to buy the video game! She is proud of herself for making good buying decisions.

Emily saved **$11.83**. She saved enough money to buy the video game!

$11.83

Tennis

$10.00

BEST VALUE

Remember that value is a combination of price, quantity, and quality. You usually can't have the best of all three. You have to decide which is most important. If you think about value, you will make good buying decisions.

LOOK FOR COUPONS

Check the newspaper or the Internet. You might find coupons for discounts at hobby and craft stores.

SHOP AT DOLLAR STORES

Dollar stores can have great deals on hobby supplies. When the price is most important, a dollar store is a good place to start.

BUY USED ITEMS

Garage sales and **thrift stores** are good places to find deals. You can sometimes find high quality items for low prices.

GLOSSARY

garage – a room or building that cars are kept in. A garage sale is a sale that takes place in a garage.

goal – something you try to get or accomplish.

option – something you can choose.

organize – to arrange things in a certain way.

personalize – to mark with your name or initials.

sketch – to draw a picture. A sketch pad is a notebook that you draw pictures in.

thrift store – a store that sells used items, especially one that is run by a charity.